Sea Life

Lobsters

Lola Schaefer

www.raintreepublishers.co.uk

Visit our website to find out more information about **Raintree** books.

To order:

☎ Phone 44 (0) 1865 888112

▤ Send a fax to 44 (0) 1865 314091

▣ Visit the Raintree Bookshop at www.raintreepublishers.co.uk to browse our catalogue and order online.

First published in Great Britain by Raintree, Halley Court, Jordan Hill, Oxford OX2 8EJ, part of Harcourt Education.
Raintree is a registered trademark of Harcourt Education Ltd.

Editorial: Nick Hunter and Diyan Leake
Design: Sue Emerson (HL-US) and Joanna Sapwell (www.tipani.co.uk)
Picture Research: Amor Montes de Oca (HL-US)
Production: Lorraine Hicks

Originated by Dot Gradations
Printed and bound in China by South China Printing Company

ISBN 1 844 21012 X
07 06 05 04 03
10 9 8 7 6 5 4 3 2 1

❗ CAUTION: Remind children that it is not a good idea to handle wild animals. Children should wash their hands with soap and water after they touch any animal.

British Library Cataloguing in Publication Data
Schaefer, Lola
Lobsters
595.3'84
A full catalogue record for this book is available from the British Library.

Acknowledgements
The publishers would like to thank the following for permission to reproduce photographs: Animals Animals p. 18 (Zig Leszczynski) Bruce Coleman Inc. p. 4 (Jane Burton), 23 (antennae and claw, Jane Burton), back cover (antennae, Jane Burton) Color Pic, Inc. pp. 1 (E. R. Degginger), 5 (E. R. Degginger), 10 (E. R. Degginger), 22 (E. R. Degginger), 23 (exoskeleton, E. R. Degginger), 24 (E. R. Degginger) Howardhall.com p. 19 (Michele Hall) Jeff Rotman Photography pp. 7, 13, 14, 15, 16 (Doug Perrine), 20, 23 (female) Jay Ireland & Georgienne E. Bradley/Bradleyireland.com p. 23 (seaweed) Jonathan Bird p. 8 ORG p. 12 (Jonathan Bird) Photo Researchers, Inc. pp. 11 (Bryan Hitchcock/National Audubon Society), 17 (Andrew J. Martinez), 21 (George D. Lepp) Robert E. Barber p. 9 Visuals Unlimited pp. 6 (Marty Snyderman), 23 (jointed leg), back cover (jointed legs), p. 15L (Peter Morris)

Cover photograph of a lobster, reproduced with permission of Bruce Coleman Inc. (Jane Burton)

Every effort has been made to contact copyright holders of any material reproduced in this book. Any omissions will be rectified in subsequent printings if notice is given to the publishers.

Some words are shown in bold, **like this**. You can find them in the glossary on page 23.

Contents

What are lobsters?

Lobsters are sea animals.

They are hard on the outside.

They do not have any bones inside.

jointed leg

Animals that do not have a backbone are called **invertebrates**.

Lobsters are invertebrates with **jointed legs**.

Where do lobsters live?

Very young lobsters float in the sea.

Adult lobsters live on the sea floor.

Some lobsters live in rocky holes.

They may live alone.

They may live with other lobsters.

What do lobsters look like?

tail

Lobsters have a long body and a long tail.

antennae

Lobsters have long **antennae** as well.

They use their antennae to feel, smell and taste food.

What kind of shells do lobsters have?

People say that lobsters have 'shells'.

Hard outsides of lobsters are really called **exoskeletons**.

old shell

As lobsters grow, their shells get too small.

They leave the old shell and grow new, bigger shells.

What do lobsters feel like?

Lobsters are bumpy and hard.

claw

Lobster **claws** are sharp.

How big are lobsters?

Young lobsters are about the size of your fingernail.

Adult lobsters can be almost as
big as you!

How do lobsters move?

Lobsters crawl on the sea floor.

Some lobsters crawl many miles.

tail

Lobsters can quickly curl their tail.

This moves them backwards.

What do lobsters eat?

Lobsters eat soft foods.

They eat fish and worms.

starfish

Lobsters eat other things in the sea.

They eat **seaweed** and starfish.

19

Where do new lobsters come from?

eggs

Female lobsters lay thousands of eggs.

The eggs stick on the mother's tail for a long time.

Then, the eggs float away.

Young lobsters come out of
the eggs.

Quiz

What are these lobster parts?

Can you find them in the book?

Look for the answers on page 24.

? ? ? ?

Glossary

antennae
long parts on an animal's head that it uses as feelers

claw
part that a lobster uses to hold things with, like a hand

exoskeleton
hard outer covering on the body of insects and some animals

female
a female parent is the mother

invertebrate
animal that has no backbone

jointed leg
leg with parts that move where they are joined together

seaweed
plant that lives in the sea

Index

Answers to quiz on page 22

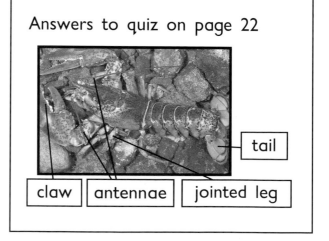

claw   antennae   jointed leg   tail

Titles in the Sea Life series include:

Hardback   1 844 21010 3

Hardback   1 844 21011 1

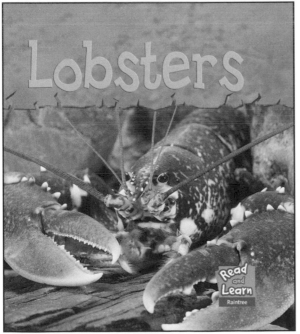

Hardback   1 844 21012 X

Hardback   1 844 21013 8

Find out about the other titles in this series on our website www.raintreepublishers.co.uk